BREED HISTORY

The history of the Persian cat is, in fact, the history of all longhaired breeds, because it is almost certainly from the Persian that all other longhaired breeds have been developed. The Balinese (longhaired Siamese) and the Somali (longhaired Abyssinian) may well be the exceptions to this statement nearby neighbors. Longhaired cats were associated with these countries from about the 16th century, and maybe even earlier. It was during that period that the first cats of this type began to arrive in Europe. There are no wild breeds of cat that sport a truly long coat so it must be assumed that this feature arose

The Persian is one of the oldest longhaired breeds of cat.

because it is thought that these breeds developed from an independent longhaired mutation in the shorthaired breeds mentioned.

When the first Persians appeared is not known, nor where they were developed. However, credit for the breed is generally given to the peoples of Turkey, Iran (formerly Persia), and their from a mutation in shorthaired cats that were possibly of Egyptian origin.

The colder winter climates of Turkey and Iran no doubt favored such a mutation. Once it appeared it would have aroused great interest among cat owners. It would also mean such cats would have had greater value than their shorthaired cousins.

The domestic cat itself, which has the scientific name of *Felis catus*, is thought to have derived from the jungle cat, *Felis chaus*, or the African wild cat, *Felis lybica*. These species are regarded by some zoologists as subspecific forms of the European wild cat, *Felis sylvestris*. If this is so, then the domestic cat is more appropriately named *Felis sylvestris catus*, a very regal-sounding name.

THE ORIGINAL PERSIANS

The Persian of today bears little resemblance to the original Persian in either its coat length, colors, or anatomy. It is the result of many years of intensive selective breeding for these features. If we could go back in time, it would be found that longhaired cats from both Persia and Turkey were shipped to Europe, where they found favor in France, in particular.

The French naturalist the Comte de Buffon wrote his *Histoire Naturelle* in 1756. In it, he refers to the text of the 16th century Italian explorer Pietro della Valla, who described the longhaired cat of the day and stated that it came from Chorazan, which is in the north of Iran. He said it was a breed with long, very fine and silky hair, especially on the tail. He also stated that it was a uniformly gray color, being darker on the head, and that such cats were very tame. Buffon noted that apart from the color, the breed was exactly the same as the cat known in France as the Angora.

The Angora was, in earlier times, a breed that was regarded as only white in color. In reality, the Angoras were (and remain so today) of many colors; however, the white ones were held in great esteem by the French and other European nobility. The Angora was native to Turkey. The famed French diplomat Cardinal Richelieu, who died in 1642, was a great cat lover. Ironically, this was at a time when the church itself was the greatest enemy of the cat and was having them thrown from towers, burnt, and in other ways cruelly treated. Richelieu owned a "chat Angora" named Lucifer, but it was black, not white. It seems that in those days, it was more a case of who owned the cat, rather than the cat itself, that determined whether felines were pure in spirit or a consort of the devil!

Be this as it may, you can see that in Europe by the time of the 19th century, there were longhaired cats that were variously called Angora or Persian according to the whims of their owners. The fact that there may have been a slight difference in both the coats and the structure of these otherwise similar breeds went unnoticed, or largely so. In point of fact, the Father of the Cat Fancy, Englishman Harrison Weir, did state late in the 19th century that many cross-bred felines were being sold as "Russian, Angoran or Persian," which clearly suggests that a distinction between the Persian and the Angora was appreciated,

Female cream Persian. Where the first Persians appeared is not known, nor where they were developed.

at least by a few cat enthusiasts. However, whether this was in respect of their origins or their type is not at all clear.

From the many paintings of cats portrayed with their owners during the 18th century we do gain a clear insight into what the original Persians looked like. They were very much like the present-day Angora. This means they had a typical feline head shape with an obvious wedged muzzle. They were of good bone structure but not massive. The coat was long and silky, being neither unduly dense nor woolly.

In 1868 Chas Ross made an interesting statement about the Persian in his *Book of Cats.* While stating, as had Buffon over a century earlier, that the Persian was a gray color, he also stated that the Persian had very long and silky fur "perhaps more so than the cat of Angora." He went on to say that the Persian was a cat of exceedingly gentle manner and probably one of the most beautiful varieties.

It would seem that in those days the main criterion of whether a cat was Persian or Angoran was in fact its color rather than its structure. However, at that time there were no cat clubs, no stud books, and no pedigrees of value. If a person was to claim a cat was Persian or Angoran, no one could really challenge this (other than via its color) because there was no standard and no way to disprove such a statement.

THE BIRTH OF THE CAT FANCY

In 1871 Harrison Weir organized the world's first cat show at the Crystal Palace in London. The phenomenal success of this show was to result in the emergence of the cat fancy as a highly organized hobby. At that first show there were Persian cats, Angoras and a French-African cat that was clearly of Persian type. However, officially, all of the longhaired cats were labeled as being "Eastern." The cats which seemed to attract the most interest were described as white Persians, which seems contradictory to the concept of Persians being gray. However, another cat of note which was claimed to have been imported directly from Persia was black, gray, and white.

It would seem that in the years that followed the London show, there are more references to the fact that the Persian should have a denser coat than the Angora and a somewhat larger and rounded head. This prompted breeders to select for these features. But it must be appreciated that prior to the beginnings of the cat fancy, there was indeed no clear-cut distinction between the Persian and the Angora, or between cats labeled as Russian or Algerian, in respect to their conformation and fur type.

Following the London show, many other exhibitions were staged with success and became popular throughout the Western world, especially so in the US. The Persian, as it was more frequently

This striking black Persian embodies all of the beautiful qualities of its breed.

described (regardless of whether it was actually Persian or Angora), was a sensation at all shows and quickly dominated all exhibitions where it invariably took the Best in Show award.

Within a relatively short span of time the Persian had become so popular that the numbers bred had produced various mutations. By 1900, the colors that were established included the black, blue, white, orange, cream, sable, smoke, tabby, and the bi- and tricolors. In 1901, the world's first longhaired cat club was formed, this being the Blue Persian Cat Society in England.

THE DEVELOPMENT OF THE PERSIAN

With the formation of cat clubs in Britain, mainland Europe, and the US, so came the beginning of stud books and the establishment of standards. The Persian was regarded as the epitome of what a longhaired cat should be. A Persian should be a big-boned feline with a dense coat, a round face and a somewhat foreshortened muzzle. This was what the standards stated. The result was that breeders concentrated on producing cats that met these criteria, which thus increased the chances of their exhibits winning awards.

The effect of this was that the Angora type lost popularity. However, before this situation was reached, there had already been so much cross breeding between Persian and Angoras that, for all practical purposes, they had become the same breed.

Eventually, the use of the term Angora was dropped altogether in the West. This meant that all longhaired cats of purebreeding lines were thus Persians and were judged against the Persian standard.

In the UK, however, the term Persian itself was to be dropped and replaced by "longhaired." In America, the Persian name was retained and persists to this day. More recently (1988) the British reintroduced the name Persian within the longhaired section of the standards.

With the passing of many years, the Persian has changed dramatically from its original type. Today it sports an extremely profuse coat which has become much more woolly and rather less silky than it was. This is because selection has been for the undercoat more than for the top coat and its guard hairs. The face is noticeably broader and the nose much more dished. Indeed, there is a variety called the Peke-faced Persian in the US, in which the nose is depressed as in the Pekingese dog. However, this variant is not recognized in Britain due to the health problems that are associated with excessive muzzle reduction.

Within the Persian breed you can see all stages of muzzle reduction. So if you prefer, as do the British, a less extreme form of the Persian face, it can still be found if you are prepared to search among stock that is not unduly exaggerated for this feature. In the same way, there

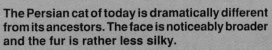

The Persian cat of today is dramatically different from its ancestors. The face is noticeably broader and the fur is rather less silky.

Blue-eyed white. Persians of this color variety can also be found with copper eyes or odd-colored eyes—one blue and one copper.

are Persians that still sport a fur which displays a quality top coat with a high sheen. The breed therefore exhibits a wide range of variables from which you can select.

The Persian of today is rather more cobby in stature than was its ancestors, and its bone structure is somewhat heavier. In terms of the colors now seen, the progress has been spectacular, from the self blacks and whites to the gorgeous shaded Persians and the cameos. You can even have a Siamese-patterned Persian in the form of the Himalayan. Some registries classify this as a separate breed because it was created by hybridization with the Siamese. But most associations accept it as a Persian because the Siamese genes have long since been bred out of it.

The character of the Persian has always been highly regarded, and it remains superb to this day. Gentle, quiet and always affectionate, the Persian is arguably the ideal breed for those who have the desire to lavish much time on their cats.

The Persian is the "aristocat" of cats. Its beauty and charm are unsurpassed.

SELECTING A PERSIAN CAT

Before discussing the matter of selecting a Persian cat or kitten, it is appropriate to offer a cautionary note. The Persian is a singularly beautiful feline with a magnificent coat. However, this coat is not self-grooming! If left unattended the Persian can look a very sorry example of a cat. The fur will mat right down to the skin. The extent of the mats will become greater every time your pet gets wet. If you are not prepared to devote at least 20 or so minutes every other day to grooming your Persian, then do not obtain an example of this breed (or indeed any longhaired breed). If you plan to exhibit your Persian, it will need grooming daily to ensure the coat remains in the best condition.

THE QUALITY OF YOUR PET

Persians come in a range of qualities from the inferior, through the typical examples of the breed, to those which are show winners, or at least potentially so. You may wish to own a high-quality Persian even though you have no intention to show it. Quality means it will have good bone conformation, the correct stature, and its color or patterns will be of a high standard. Such a cat will be a costly purchase. A typical Persian will be just that. It will display no glaring faults and its color will be sound. It may display some minor failings in type or color that would preclude it from ever being of show quality.

An inferior Persian will be one which has obvious faults, either its conformation, its coat quality, poor color or in other ways inferior. Such cats are often described as being pet quality. As long as you appreciate that this term means inferior, its use is fine. However, there are two kinds of inferior Persians. There is the cat which is inferior only in respect to its type and color—not in relation to its basic structure and health.

There is then the inferior cat produced by those who are in Persians just to make money. These people have cats that they breed with no consideration for the vigor of the offspring. Such kittens are invariably sickly and prone to illnesses throughout their lives. Poor health and inferior Persians result from unplanned matings and excessive breeding, coupled with a lack of ongoing selection being applied to future breeding stock.

How do you make the right choice when selecting a Persian? The answer is you do your homework. Visit shows, talk to established exhibitors, and judges. When you visit the seller take a good look at his stock, and more especially the living conditions of the cats. Is he giving you the hard sell, or does he seem more concerned about the kitten's future home? Sometimes the dedicated seller might even annoy you, but he is concerned for his kittens, even if they are not quality Persians. The more Persians you see, the more likely you are to make a wise choice.

tends to be much the same from one day to the next, whatever his character might be.

It really is a pot-luck matter just how affectionate a kitten will grow up to become. Cats are very much individuals, and they can change as they grow up. The way

Copper-eyed whites. The appearance of the Persian cat today is the result of many years of intensive selective breeding.

WHICH SEX TO PURCHASE?

From the viewpoint of pet suitability, there really is no difference between a tom (male) and a queen (female). Some people prefer one sex, but this is purely subjective. This author has found males to be more consistent in their character than females, who may tend to be "all or nothing" in their attitude. In other words, they can be extremely affectionate one day, but rather standoffish the next. The tom

they are treated also affects their personality. Therefore, it is more a case of selecting a kitten that appeals to you, regardless of its sex.

Of course, if you wish to become a breeder then the female has to be the better choice. Once she reaches breeding age you can then select a suitable mate for her from the hundreds of quality stud males available to you. If you purchase a male with the view to owning a stud, you are really

This Persian kitten already sports a thick, lush coat. Like other breeds of cat—including shorthaired ones—Persians periodically shed hair.

gambling that he will mature into a fine cat that others would want to use. For this to happen, your tom would need to be very successful in the show ring, and then in the quality of his offspring.

Furthermore, owning a whole tom (a male that has not been neutered) does present more practical problems than owning a queen. Such a male will be continually marking his territory (your furniture) by spraying it with his urine, which is hardly a fragrant scent!

If your Persian is to be a pet only, then regardless of the sex you should have it neutered or spayed. It will be more affectionate to you, will not be wandering off looking for romance, and will not shed its coat as excessively as would an unaltered Persian. In the case of a tom, he will not come home with

Persian and its Poodle pal. Contrary to popular belief, cats and dogs can get along well if they are introduced at an early age.

pieces of his ears missing as a result of his fights with other entire males. Your queen will not present you with kittens that you do not want but which she will have if she is not spayed. She is far less likely to spray than is the male, but she will show her desire to mate, both with her "calling" sounds, which can be eerie, and her provocative crouching position in which she is clearly inviting a mating.

WHAT AGE TO PURCHASE?

Breeders vary in the age they judge a kitten ready for a new home. An important consideration is obviously if the new owners have experience of cats generally and kittens in particular. While an eight-week-old baby is quite delightful, it is invariably better

Persians love all of the comforts of home, and a favorite chair is a must!

Tortie Persian. A cat carrier is a must for every cat owner. It will enable your pet to travel safely and comfortably.

A beautifully groomed copper-eyed white kitten. If you are not prepared to spend at least 20 or so minutes every other day on grooming, then the Persian, or any other longhaired breed, is not the one for you.

The personality of the Persian has always been highly regarded. Persians are gentle, quiet felines...a delight to own.

from a health standpoint that the kitten remains with its mother until it is ten or more weeks of age. Some breeders will not part with a kitten until it is 16 weeks of age.

The kitten should have received at least temporary vaccinations against feline distemper and rabies (if applicable in your country and if the kitten is over 12 weeks of age) and preferably protection against other major feline infections. Additionally, you should let your own vet examine your Persian.

Although most owners will wish to obtain a kitten, a potential breeder or exhibitor may find that a young adult (over eight to nine months of age) is more suitable to his needs. By this age the quality of the Persian is becoming more apparent. However, bear in mind that a mature Persian queen will not be at her peak until she is about two years of age. A tom will be even later in reaching full maturity, and he may not peak until he is five years of age.

ONE OR TWO PERSIANS?

Without any doubt, two kittens are always preferred to one. They provide constant company for each other and are a delight to watch as they play. The extra costs involved in their upkeep are unlikely to be a factor if you are able to afford a Persian in the first place.

THE PERSIAN STANDARD & COLORS

In order to determine the relative quality of a Persian cat, or any other feline, there must be a standard against which the individual can be compared. The standards are prepared by a panel of experts within each cat registration body. Periodically these descriptive documents are amended to take account of progress within the breed, or to place more emphasis on a given aspect that may be regressing. The standard can never be precise, so is open to interpretation.

Within each standard, points are allocated to various features based on their believed importance within the breed. Any person who has aspirations to exhibit, judge, or breed Persians should have a knowledge of the standard. Only by constantly referring to it can a mental picture be developed of an outstanding Persian.

To the beginner almost any Persian would seem to be a fine example when they compare it to the standard. The interpretation of the standard becomes meaningful only when combined with the experience of viewing poor, through mediocre, to those adjudged to be outstanding examples of the breed.

THE PERSIAN STANDARD

The standard quoted in this text is that of the Cat Fanciers Association of America (CFA) and is reproduced by courtesy of that Association. The CFA is the largest registration organization in the US and the one most Americans will join. Only the standard in respect of conformation is reproduced in its entirety. The colors and pattern are discussed in a general manner, thus not as written in the CFA standard. This is to avoid unnecessary duplication of words.

In Great Britain, there are only two registration bodies and of them the Governing Council of the Cat Fancy (GCCF) is easily the most important, and is also the oldest registry in the world.

If you plan to breed Persians, you are strongly recommended to do so only with registered individuals. You should obtain the show standards for the registry you plan to support. The standards are not reproduced individually but within booklets that cover all breeds recognized by the registry in question.

Point Score of the CFA

Head (including size and shape of eyes, ear shape and set): 30

Type (including shape, size, bone, and length of tail): 20

Coat: 10

Balance: 5

The Persian's beautiful eyes are a hallmark of its breed. They are brilliant in color, large, round, and full.

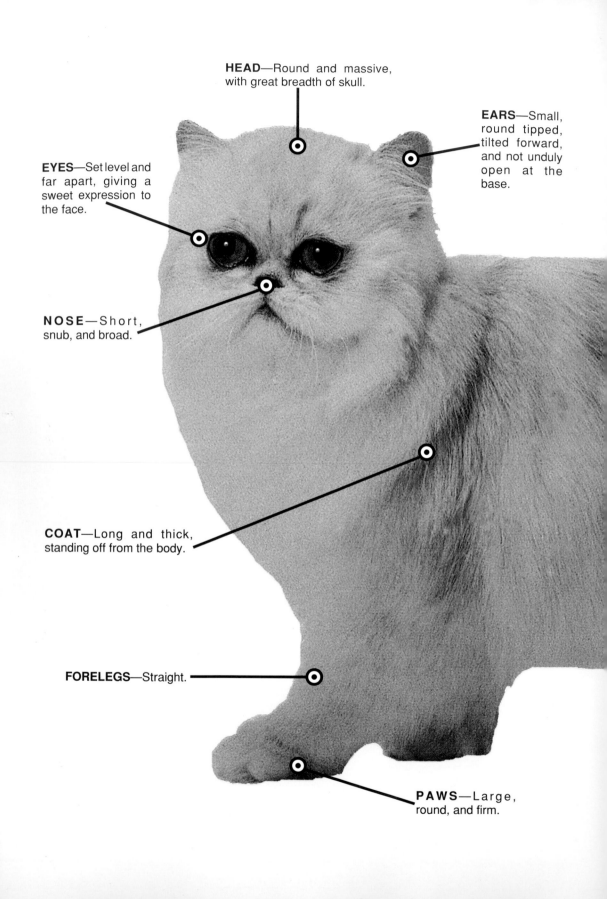

HEAD—Round and massive, with great breadth of skull.

EARS—Small, round tipped, tilted forward, and not unduly open at the base.

EYES—Set level and far apart, giving a sweet expression to the face.

NOSE—Short, snub, and broad.

COAT—Long and thick, standing off from the body.

FORELEGS—Straight.

PAWS—Large, round, and firm.

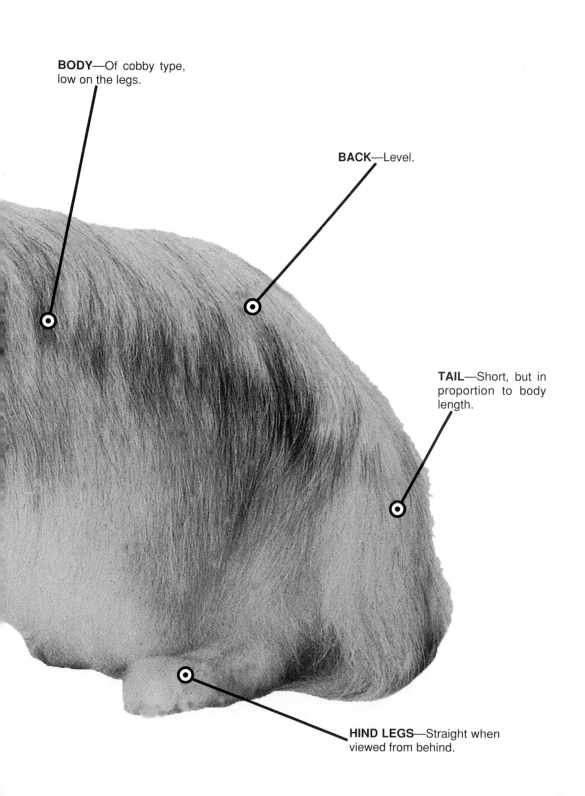

BODY—Of cobby type, low on the legs.

BACK—Level.

TAIL—Short, but in proportion to body length.

HIND LEGS—Straight when viewed from behind.

Refinement: 5
Color: 20
Eye Color: 10
Total: 100

In all tabby varieties, the 20 points for color are to be divided, 10 for markings and 10 for color. In all "with white" varieties (calico, dilute calico, bi-color, van calico, van dilute calico, and tabby and white), the 20 points for color are to be divided, 10 for "with white" pattern and 10 for color.

Head: round and massive, with great breadth of skull. Round face with round underlying bone structure. Well set on short, thick neck.

Nose: short, snub, and broad. With "break."

Cheeks: full.

Jaws: broad and powerful.

Chin: full, well-developed, and firmly rounded, reflecting a proper bite.

Ears: small, round tipped, tilted forward, and not unduly open at base. Set far apart, and low on the head, fitting into (without distorting) the rounded contour of the head.

Eyes: large, round, and full. Set far apart and brilliant, giving a sweet expression to the face.

Body: of cobby type, low on the legs, deep in the chest, equally massive across the shoulders and rump, with a short, well-rounded middle piece. Good muscle tone with no evidence of obesity. Large or medium in size. Quality the determining consideration rather than size.

Back: level.

Legs: short, thick, and strong. Forelegs straight.

Paws: large, round, and firm. Toes carried close, five in front and four behind.

Tail: short, but in proportion to body length. Carried without a curve and at an angle lower than the back.

Coat: long and thick, standing off from the body. Of fine texture, glossy and full of life. Long all over the body, including the shoulders. The ruff immense and continuing in a deep frill between the front legs. Ear and toe tufts long. Brush very full.

Disqualify: locket or button. Kinked or abnormal tail. Incorrect number of toes. Any apparent weakness in hind quarters. Any apparent deformity of the spine. Deformity of the skull resulting in an asymmetrical face and/or head. For pointed cats, also disqualify for crossed eyes, white toes, eye color other than blue.

PERSIAN COLORS

The CFA recognizes some 42 color and pattern combinations in the Persian, which should be more than enough for you to select from.

It is beyond the scope of this book to discuss in detail all of the Persian colors, so what follows is a general overview. Colors and patterns can be conveniently divided into groups and they are the selfs, bicolors, shaded, pointed, tabbies, and tortoiseshells (torties). Each group attracts its own devotees.

Selfs

A self color is a single color that will produce itself when two

Persians displaying the color are mated. All self colors should be even and display no marks, patterns, ticks or tendencies to change color at their roots. This is not always possible with dark selfs because they are subject to the bleaching action of the sun. Black, in particular, is an extremely difficult "color" to breed to a high standard of excellence (yet it is achieved). Selfs must be free of other colored hairs, but in blacks the odd white hair may be seen on a kitten which often disappears as the kitten matures. The self colors are the following:

White: Pure glistening white. The eye color is blue or copper, (which you can also read in all instances as deep orange).

However, you can have an odd-eyed white which will have one blue and one copper-colored eye.

Black: Dense coal-black free of rusty tinge. Eyes copper.

Shaded silver Persian. This variety has a white undercoat with a mantle of black tipping shading down from sides, face, and tail from dark on the ridge to white on the chin, chest, stomach, and undertail.

Blue: Lighter shade preferred, but an even dark blue is better than an uneven lighter shade.

Red: Deep and rich. Lips and chin to match color. Eyes copper.

Cream: Buff cream, lighter shades preferred. Eyes copper.

Chocolate: rich, warm chocolate brown—medium to dark. Eyes copper.

Lilac: rich warm lavender with a pinkish hue. Eyes copper.

Bicolors

These are two-colored Persians in which one of the colors is white. The requirements in the US and Britain differ so both are quoted.

The CFA states: As a preferred minimum, the cat should have white feet, legs, undersides, chest

The "break" of the nose should be centered between the eyes.

and muzzle. Less than this minimum should be penalized proportionately. Inverted "V" blaze on face desirable. Eyes copper.

The GCCF requires: The patches of colour to be clear, even and well distributed. Not more than two-thirds of the cat's coat to be coloured and not more than one-half to be white. Face to be patched with color and white. Eyes copper.

Given the fact that the white areas on the bicolor are the result of random expression of the white spotting gene, it is probably easier to produce a show bicolor in the UK than in the US. However, in both countries the placement of the white is a matter of luck rather than breeder control.

The recognized solid color elements of the bicolors are black, blue, red or cream (CFA) to which the GCCF additionally accepts chocolate or lilac. The Van bicolor is a white cat in which the color is restricted to the head, tail and legs as in the Turkish Van breed.

Shaded Patterns

The various shaded patterns in the Persian are quite exquisite. There are smokes, shaded and shells; they differ in the extent of color tipping to each hair follicle. The result is a series of shadings that go from dark to light in the following order.

Smoke: in this the color extends well down the shaft so that the lighter or white color below is not

Keystone Juniper, a red and white female, in her kittening box.

The Persian's coat is fine in texture, glossy, and full of life.

seen until the cat actually moves or the hair is parted. However, the hair is darker on the head, back, and feet, so that the smoke does display contrasting lighter and darker patterns of color. The smokes of the red series are often referred to as cameo. The smoke colors are black, blue, cream, blue-cream (dilute tortoiseshell), chocolate, lilac, and tabby. Eye color copper.

Shaded: in this pattern the undercoat is again white or very light in color, but the extent of tipping is less than in the smokes. The result is a lighter appearance than in the smokes. The colors are silver (blue-green eyes), pewter (orange eyes), golden (eyes green or blue-green), red (cameo), and tortoiseshell, eyes copper on the last two colors.

Shell: this is the lightest of the shaded patterns and for many is the most beautiful because of the delicacy of the shading. Only the very tips of the hair are pigmented. The colors are cameo (red), chinchilla (white with black tips), chinchilla golden (warm beige with chocolate or black tips), and tortie (white base with black tips and patches of red and cream). Eye color: tortie and red are copper, the others blue or blue-green.

Pointed Pattern

In Britain the pointed pattern is known as the Colourpoint Longhair, while in the US it is called the Himalayan for the similar pattern seen in rabbits, guinea pigs, mice and other small mammals. It is, of course, the familiar pattern of the Siamese breed, from which it was transferred to Persians by hybridization. The basis of the pointed pattern is that the mask, feet, tail and ears are pigmented in a color, while the rest of the body is of a much lighter shade of the pointed color.

lighter. Not all cats are affected by the same temperatures because the "trigger" that prompts a change in color is determined by genes on an individual basis.

There are many colors and patterns available in pointed Persians and among them are the following: seal (a dark brown); chocolate (milk); blue; lilac; flame (red); cream; tortie in its various colors; tabby in its various colors; and tortie-tabbies in a range of

Dilute calico Persian. There is a wide variety of bi-color Persians, each of which is equally attractive.

An interesting feature of the pointed pattern is that it is thermosensitive. This means that it is affected by the ambient temperature. In cool climates the points become a darker color, while in hot climates they become

colors. The tabby point is often referred to in the US as the lynx point.

The Tabby Pattern
The tabby pattern is seen in two of its three variations in the

Persian and other breeds. The mackerel tabby is that of the wild cat, named for the three central lines of black on the back, and the lines that extend down the flanks. The legs are ringed with black, as is the tail. The classic or blotched tabby features large blotches or spirals of black on the body, rather than stripes. In both varieties the head features the characteristic "M" on the forehead, and necklaces on the neck and chest. The abdomen is spotted.

The dark stripes contrast with the paler ground color. Without doubt the classic tabby is the more easily seen pattern in a longcoated cat like the Persian. It is seen at its best when there is a

Blue-cream Persian. This variety is blue with patches of cream or softly intermingled areas of cream on both body and extremities.

Blue Persian. In this variety, a lighter shade is preferred. The color should be one level tone from nose to tip of tail.

stark contrast between the tabby markings and the ground color, for example, in the silver tabby where the ground is silver and the markings are black. The brown tabby has a sable or copper ground with black markings, while the blue tabby has pale blue ground with dark blue stripes. There are also red, cameo (a lighter shade of red with off-white ground), and cream tabbies. Eye color is copper.

There is a tortie tabby, which is known as the torbie or patched. This is a tabby in any of its colors with the addition of red or cream patches. The tabby pattern is often referred to in the US as the tiger pattern by those not familiar with pattern names. Note that in tabbies the color of the variety is

A pet-quality Persian kitten. Persians of this type can make as good a pet as those that are of show quality.

taken from the ground color, not the markings, which are black, or a darker shade of the ground color, depending on the variety. You can also have a tabby and white Persian. In this variety the white should appear as defined in the bicolor text.

Tortoiseshell Pattern

This is a tricolored pattern and is a female-only combination. The colors are black, red, and cream, and they should be well defined and spread over the body. Eyes are copper. The chocolate tortie has this color replacing the black. The dilute tortie is known as the blue-cream, and the blue replaces the black while the red becomes a cream. The tortoiseshell and white of Britain is known as the calico in the US, and its dilution is the dilute calico (blue-cream). Eye color is copper.

Five-month-old red Persian.

FEEDING YOUR PERSIAN

Cats and kittens are very much like people when it comes to their eating habits. Some are extremely easy to satisfy; others are much more difficult to please. Adult cats can be a worry, but at least you know they must have eaten something to have survived to maturity. Kittens, on the other hand, can prematurely turn your hair gray because you fear they may not thrive unless you can come up with some delicacy that tempts their palate!

Fortunately, there are so many quality brands of commercial cat foods available today that it should be possible to get even the most fastidious of kittens through its most difficult early months.

Waiting to be fed...With the wide variety of commercial cat foods that are on the market, even the most finicky cat will be encouraged to eat.

CATS ARE CARNIVORES

The cat is a prime predator in its wild habitat, and this means its basic diet must be composed of the flesh of other animals, be they mammals, birds, or fish. The digestive tract of a carnivore has evolved to cope with proteins, but it has little ability to digest raw vegetable matter. This means the latter must first be boiled, so that the hard cellulose walls of such foods are softened, then broken down by the digestive juices and flora found in the alimentary tract.

In the wild, the cat would eat just about every part of its prey, leaving only the bones that were too large for it to digest. This diet would provide proteins and fats from the body tissues, roughage from the fur or feathers, and carbohydrates and vitamins from the partially digested vegetable matter that would be in the intestines of the prey. Combined with water, a very well-balanced diet would be provided for the cat. An equivalent of such nutrition is what you must strive to supply.

COMMERCIAL FOODS

The range of commercial cat foods encompasses canned, semi-moist, and dry diets. We have always found that our cats have never really enjoyed any of the semi-moist foods. The canned and dry foods come in an extensive range of flavors, which include meat, fish, and poultry. Of the canned foods, some have a firm consistency; others are chunks in a sauce. There are also formulated kitten foods.

Commercial foods can form the basis of your Persian's diet, but you should supply a variety of them to reduce the chances that some key constituent is missing from the diet. Persians will no doubt help in this matter because they seem to tire of one brand if it is fed daily. Indeed, deciding which is their chosen flavor of the week can be an interesting guessing game. They will suddenly show no interest in a product they seemed to eat with relish just a few days earlier! You will find that some cats enjoy fish flavors, others poultry and yet others, the various meats.

Dry food is enjoyed by most, though not all, Persians. It provides good exercise for the teeth and jaw muscles, which canned foods do not. Their other advantage is that you can leave them out all day without their losing their appeal to your pets, or attracting flies. Water must always be available to your cats; this is even more important if the basic diet is of dried foods.

NON-COMMERCIAL FOODS

Your Persian will enjoy many of the foods that you eat. These foods provide both variety and good exercise for the jaws. Human consumption meats can be of beef, pork, or lamb. All fish should be steamed or boiled, and it is best to stay with white fish such as cod. Tuna, sardines, and other canned fish are appreciated, but only give small quantities of them as a treat because they may prove too rich for your pet's system. Chicken is enjoyed by nearly all cats.

Cheese, egg yolk, spaghetti, and even boiled rice are all items that you can offer to your pets to see if it appeals to them. Small beef and other meat bones that still have some meat on them will be enjoyed and keep a kitten or cat amused for quite some time. Beware of bones that easily splinter, such as those of chicken or rabbit.

You can by all means see if small pieces of vegetables or fruits are accepted if mixed with the food, but generally cats will leave them. This is no problem, providing that the cat is receiving commercial foods as its basic diet. Such products are all fortified with essential vitamins after the cooking process.

HOW MUCH TO FEED?

Cats prefer to eat a little but often, rather than consume one mighty meal a day. However, as carnivores, adults are well able to cope with one large meal a day. The same is not true of kittens, which should receive three or four meals per day. A kitten or a cat will normally only consume that which is needed. You can arrive at this amount by trial and error. If kitty devours its meal and is looking for more, then let it have more. You will quickly be able to judge how much each kitten needs to satisfy itself. Always remove any moist foods that are uneaten after each meal.

At 12 weeks of age the kitten should have four meals a day. One of these meals can be omitted when the kitten is 16 weeks old, but increase the quantity of the other three. You can reduce to two meals a day when the kitten is about nine months of age. From that age, it is best to continue feeding two meals—one in the morning and one in the early evening. How many times a day you feed your adult cat is unimportant. The key factor is that it receives as much as it needs over the day, and that the diet is balanced to provide the essential ingredients discussed earlier. It is also better that meals are given regularly. Cats, like humans, are creatures of habit.

WATER

If a cat's diet is essentially of moist foods, it will drink far less than if the diet is basically of dry foods. Many cats do not like faucet (tap) water because they are able to smell and taste the many additives included by your local water board. Chlorine is high on this list. Although it dissipates into the air quite readily, chloromides do not, which is why the cat may ignore the water. During the filtering process at the water station, chemicals are both taken out and added. The resulting mineral balance and taste is often not to a cat's liking. This is why you will see cats drinking from puddles, a flower vase, or even your toilet,

The adult Persian can be fed once daily, or the meal can be divided and offered in the morning and the evening. The important thing is to establish a regular feeding schedule and stick to it.

because the taste is better for them. If your water is refused, then you can see if your cat prefers mineralized bottled water—not distilled because the latter has no mineral content to it.

THE NEW ARRIVAL

It is a very traumatic time for a kitten when it leaves its mother and siblings. It will often eat well the first day; however, as it starts to miss its family, it will fret. You can reduce its stress by providing the diet it was receiving from the seller. You can change the diet slowly, if necessary, as it settles down. Of course, many kittens have no problems, but if yours does, this feeding advice should help its period of adjustment.

What is essential is that the kitten takes in sufficient liquids so that it does not start to dehydrate. This, more than anything else, will adversely affect its health very rapidly. If you are at all concerned, do consult your vet. The kitten may have picked up a virus, but if it is treated promptly, this should not be a problem. Your vet might supply you with a dietary supplement, which we have found excellent for kittens experiencing "new home syndrome."

GENERAL CARE & GROOMING

In order to properly care for your Persian kitten, it is advisable to purchase certain essential items before it arrives in your home. You will want at least one large litter tray. If it is too small, you will only need a bigger one later. Trays can be of the simple open style or domed to retain the odor within them. You can also purchase a litter tray curtain so that the tray is discreetly hidden yet accessible for your kitty. You will need a bag of cat litter as well.

Your Persian and just about any other cat will appreciate a nice soft cat bed. Pet shops stock cat beds in a number of different styles.

Another essential item will be a scratching post, otherwise your cat will shred your furniture. Posts come in a range of styles—from those that are fitted to the wall to the freestanding models that can be simple or very complex climbing frames. A third essential will be a cat carrier, which can be fiberglass or of the metal cage type. Apart from being a means of transporting kitty to the vet, it also doubles as a bed and a place to confine a kitten if necessary.

You will need a soft hand brush, preferably of natural bristle not nylon, as well as one or more combs. Again, nylon is not the best choice for a comb because it generates static electricity that causes the hair to "fly." One comb should be wide-toothed, the other medium or narrow. As the kitty grows up, an extra brush of a more stiff bristle type will be required. Although it may not be needed initially, you will eventually need an elasticized cat collar and name tag.

You will also need feeding utensils: a food bowl and water bowl. There is a wide variety of them available at pet shops. Finally, your new kitten will enjoy play toys. Balls and "squeaky" mice seem to be favorites with many cats.

SAFETY PRECAUTIONS

Before the kitten arrives in your home, check that there are no safety hazards. An open balcony is an obvious risk, as are any trailing electrical wires that are always left in their sockets. A washing machine with the door left open is a tempting place for a kitten to take a catnap. Always be careful where open doors and windows are concerned. Apart

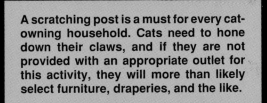

A scratching post is a must for every cat-owning household. Cats need to hone down their claws, and if they are not provided with an appropriate outlet for this activity, they will more than likely select furniture, draperies, and the like.

from the kitten running out if the door is an outside exit, there is the danger of doors slamming on the kitten.

Be very careful when kitty is in the kitchen and you are working. They have a habit of always being under your feet as you turn round. Should you be carrying a boiling hot saucepan, this could be a real danger for you and the kitten. Likewise, never leave an iron on its board. Should you be called to the telephone, you can just bet that this will be the time that kitty will decide to climb the trailing wire and cause the iron to tumble over. All open and electrical fireplaces should, of course, be fitted with a mesh guard.

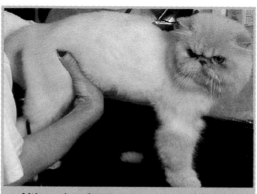

Although a show-cat owner would never attempt to trim down a Persian, some pet owners may choose a summer clip or a lion clip, which this Persian is sporting.

If you keep fish, be sure the tank hood is secure so that the kitten cannot knock it off and fall in the water. Indoor plants are best kept well out of kitty's reach. Apart from damaging them, some could prove poisonous if the leaves were nibbled. Any cherished ornaments should also be placed well away from a kitten.

SLEEPING ARRANGEMENTS

Your kitten will be happy to sleep anywhere that is cozy, warm, and draft-free. This can be in a cat basket; its carrier, in which a soft blanket has been placed; on a chair; or best of all, on your bed. If you are the kind of person who does not look kindly on cats sleeping on your chairs or other furniture, the best advice I can give you is to forget about owning a cat!

If you wish to restrict the rooms where your cat may sleep, the simple solution is to be sure the doors are closed to those rooms. If you allow your kitten to sleep on your bed, do this only if you intend to let it do so once it is grown up; otherwise, it is unfair. Kittens really love sleeping with their owners, and they are no trouble at all—quite the opposite. They will amuse you with their antics.

LITTER TRAINING

Cats are extremely clean and fastidious in all aspects of their personal habits. Kittens are easily litter box trained, providing certain fundamentals are observed. The first of these is that cats do not like to attend to their toiletry needs in an already fouled litter box. Be sure fecal matter is always removed once you that see the kitten has used the litter box. Disinfect the litter box every few days so that it does not become smelly.

Litter training is accomplished simply by placing the kitten in the litter box every time it looks as though it wants to relieve itself. Such times will be whenever it wakes up, after it has eaten, and after it has been playing a while. One warning sign is the kitty turning in circles or searching for a corner while mewing.

Approach the kitten without alarming it and quickly transfer it to the litter box. Once this has been done on one or two occasions, the kitten will go to the litter box by itself. The main litter box is normally placed near the kitchen door. It is then a case of ensuring that it is kept clean. If the kitten roams freely indoors, you can place another litter box at a strategic point. Never admonish a kitten should it make the odd mistake, as this will prove counterproductive. Rarely will such a situation occur with a litter-trained kitten, unless the youngster is feeling ill or has loose bowels. Remember, kittens can control their bowels only for a few seconds. Total control comes, as with humans, with maturity.

Your Persian will enjoy playing with a variety of toys, especially those that are small enough to be batted around.

GENERAL TRAINING

Cats live for the moment; they do not relate the past with the present, but draw from it via their memory to determine a course of present action. An example will illustrate this point. If you call your pet to you and then discipline it for doing something in the past, whether this was minutes before or days before, the cat will relate only to what is happening at that moment.

Any discipline imposed out of context, i.e., the time and place of the offense, will be meaningless. Any discipline must therefore occur at the moment of the misdemeanor, otherwise the two things will not be connected in the mind of your Persian. If your cat is scratching the furniture, simply shout "no" if you cannot get to it and take it to the scratching post. It will associate the harsh "no" with the act of scratching the furniture, which is what you want. When you see it scratching its post, you praise it, and it will register in its mind that scratching this particular object pleases you. Training is as simple as that and only becomes difficult after a cat has been allowed to acquire bad habits.

CATS AND OTHER PETS

Kittens, in particular, will get along well with other cats and other pets if they are introduced to them at a young age. However, potential prey species are not included. Never leave a cat alone with a mouse, gerbil, hamster, small bird, baby rabbits, or guinea pigs. If it doesn't kill them, it will either maul them or frighten them. Where dogs are concerned, you must watch how the dog reacts and always be present until you know they are compatible.

When kittens are introduced into a home that already has an adult cat, the cat may be curious or hostile.

However, its hostility will only take the form of spitting at the kitten or maybe cuffing it around the head with a sheathed paw. How soon it accepts the kitten can range from hours to months. Some adults will become very friendly with a kitten as it matures, others will tolerate it without ever wishing to socialize too much. Always lavish extra praise on the resident pet so that it never becomes jealous of the new interloper.

GROOMING

Daily, or at the least every other day, grooming is essential if you own a Persian or any other longhaired cat. If your pet is given access to the outdoors, the coat will become tangled and matted without daily grooming. Remember, a long coat is not natural for a cat. Burrs, grasses, leaves, and any number of foreign bodies will cling to a long coat and be the source of problems. Cuts, sores, and lumps are not easily seen in a Persian and can escape your attention unless you are grooming on a regular basis.

Begin as soon as you obtain your kitten. This will soon become a familiar event to the kitty. Providing you go about it in a gentle manner, it should become a pleasurable experience. Always begin by using your brush with the lie of the fur and then against it. This removes any objects in the fur and untangles the coat. Next use the wide-toothed comb. If you feel a mat, do not pull at it but tease it apart with your fingers, then brush it, then comb again. Repeat this process until all of the hair has been groomed.

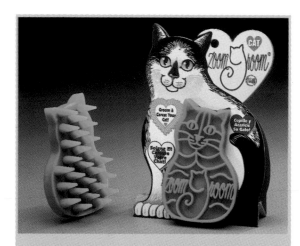

Good grooming habits should start at an early age. Your pet shop can help you select the proper grooming aids for your cat. Photo courtesy of The Kong Company.

Now you can use your narrow-toothed comb to complete the grooming; do this in the same manner as with the other comb. Finish with a brisk brushing. Always take special care when combing down the legs, the tail, and the underbelly, as they are especially sensitive parts. Your pet will resent any undue pressure on them. Brush and comb the face carefully and very gently.

While grooming, take the opportunity to inspect the skin, the ears, teeth, and between the paws. In the skin, you are looking for parasites, such as fleas or lice, or for cuts and abrasions. In the paw pads, you are looking for sores or any foreign bodies that might cause an abscess. When your Persian has a bath, it might be useful to have another family member help you. Be very sure that the cat has been well groomed before it is bathed; otherwise, mats will form that are better cut off. Be sure the water is only lukewarm, never hot or cold. Avoid getting shampoo in the ears or eyes. Use a shampoo formulated for cats.

Soak the hair thoroughly, then rub in the shampoo. Make sure that all the shampoo is rinsed from the coat; otherwise, it might irritate the skin when it dries. In any case, dry shampoo in the coat will make it sticky and will result in a lackluster appearance rather than a silky sheen. Finally, give the cat a brisk toweling, let it dry in a warm environment, and then groom it to remove any tangles that may have formed.

HANDLING CATS

If you have children, it is most important that they are instructed in the correct way to handle and appreciate their new pet. First of all, the kitten's privacy must be respected. Never let children wake up a sleeping kitten, because the kitty needs its sleep just as children do. Never let children play too roughly with a kitten, nor for an extended period of time. Cats like to play in short bursts. Always be sure that children never place elastic bands or string around the neck of a kitten, and never allow children to engage in a pulling match when a kitty has hold of a piece of string. This could get caught on their fragile teeth and damage or even pull one out.

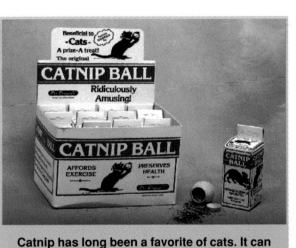

Catnip has long been a favorite of cats. It can be purchased in a variety of forms. Photo courtesy of Dr. A.C. Daniels.

Finishing touches...Here, a soft toothbrush is used to groom the hair on the face.

shoulders to secure it. It can now be lifted and firmly but gently held to your chest while the hand securing its neck will be free to stroke it. A kitten or cat must never be lifted by its front legs, nor by the loose fur on its neck. When placing a kitten back on the floor, be sure it is held securely until it is at ground level. If it feels insecure, it will try to jump. In the process it could scratch you and hurt itself if it lands awkwardly.

The correct way to lift a kitten is to place your hand underneath its chest. Next you can place your free hand on its neck, throat, or

A Persian's coat is long all over the body, including the shoulders. The ruff, which is the hair that encircles the head, is immense and continues in a deep frill between the front legs.

Male and female copper-eyed whites. Persians of either sex make equally good pets.

PRACTICAL BREEDING

Unless you wish to become a serious breeder or breeder/exhibitor, there is little point in letting your Persian female have kittens simply to reproduce her own kind. There are no benefits at all in letting her have just one litter as is sometimes stated. If your queen has been purchased as a pet, then have her spayed as soon as she is old enough, which is about 16 weeks of age (a month or so older for a tom).

BREEDING QUALITY

If you do decide to become a breeder, your objective must first and foremost be with respect to health and vigor. This means that your female should have no record of continual illnesses, nor display any known genetic faults or abnormalities. She must be maintained in healthy condition and not be allowed to become obese, as this will merely create birth difficulties.

Breeding your pet is a matter deserving of serious consideration. A good breeding program requires considerable resources of time and money.

Four-week-old white Persians. Persian litters have ranged from as small as one to as large as 14, but the average is three to five.

She should not display any recognized breed faults, such as kinks in the tail, a squint, or poor coat color. You will obviously be trying to produce kittens that are at least as good, but preferably better, than their parents.

BREEDING FACTS

The female Persian may come into a breeding state at any time after the age of four months, though it would of course be foolish to allow such a queen to have kittens when she is still so young. The youngest age that you should allow a queen to be mated is when she is 12 months old. A female cat is referred to as being polyestrus, which means she has many breeding cycles within a single year. She will tend to have two main breeding periods: in the early spring and then again in the summer.

During her seasons, she will come into heat about every 14-21 days, and will be receptive for mating for 3-6 days. This cycle will continue until she is mated—with maybe a short break during the peak of summer, and a longer one during the colder winter months. However, the normal cycles of the wild cat, which are geared to the warmer weather and the availability of ample prey species, do get distorted under domestic conditions. This is due both to artificial lighting and heating.

The cat is an induced ovulator, which means she releases eggs for fertilization only as a direct response to the stimulus of the male penis. Unlike the situation in dogs, where once a mating takes place there can be no further fertilizations (only in abnormal instances), this is not so in the cat. This means it is possible, though not common, for a litter to be sired by two or more males. After the first mating, the queen may stay in estrus for a day or two longer and can thus be mated again if she is still in the mood. It is therefore wise to ensure that a mated female is kept indoors for a few days.

A queen may have a number of litters in a year. It is advisable to restrict the number to two if you want your female to retain good health and breeding vigor, and the kittens to be healthy as well. The gestation period (the time between fertilization of an egg and the birth of the kittens) can range from 59-72 days, with 63-65 being typical. Litters born toward either extreme are likely to be associated with problem births and a number of stillborn offspring.

The size of a litter can be 1-14, the higher number having been recorded in a Persian. An average would be three to five. The queen has four pairs of teats and nurses the kittens for about five to eight weeks, though she is capable of nursing for a longer period. The kittens are born blind and helpless but are able to crawl around within a matter of days. Their eyes begin to open by about the 8th day and should be fully open by the 15th.

Once the kittens are about three weeks of age, they are able to cope with very small pieces of solid foods such as shredded meat and commercial kitten foods. The teeth of a kitten start to erupt when the youngster is two to three weeks of age. Eruption begins with the incisors and progresses backward, so that the premolars are in place by about four to six weeks. Kittens have no molars; all of their teeth are deciduous and replaced by permanent teeth by the age of about six months.

FEATURES

The initial eye color of a kitten can change quite a bit as the kitten matures, but the final color should be evident by six months. It will not, of course, change from one color to another; only the intensity and shade of the color change. The fur of a kitten grows rapidly but can take until the third year before it reaches its full maturity.

The color of a kitten will usually be darker when it is younger because the tips will be pigmented, and it is those that will be seen first. The smoke is therefore a slow—developing color. Pointed Persians are not born with pigmented points, as they are thermosensitive. The pigment develops as the kitten starts to move about in the cooler air outside its mother's womb. In this variety, the points will get progressively darker as the cat matures.

THE MATING

You are advised to plan your matings well ahead of time. You need to be satisfied that the correct tom has been chosen and that it will be available at the specified time. Do not assume that every stud owner will be prepared to let their best male cover your queen just because you are paying them a fee. The reputation of a stud is built as

percent of the offspring's genes, may simply be a bad producer herself.

When it is time for the mating, the queen is always taken to the stud. You will be able to ascertain this time because your queen will start "calling" and taking up the mating position. She is quite provocative at this time, and if you run your hand down her back, she will invariably lie down

A red tabby queen watches over her three-day-old offspring. In general, female Persian cats make good mothers.

much by the quality of offspring it sires as by its own appearance. This means such a stud owner may be very selective in only letting his top males mate with queens of quality.

All too often a stud animal takes an unfair share of the blame when poor-quality offspring are produced. He may, indeed, not be a prepotent male for his qualities, but equally true is the fact that the female, who contributes 50

with her rear end pointing upward. She is normally left with the stud owner for a few days, because at first she may lose interest in being mated due to the new surroundings. This is especially so with a maiden queen, which should, of course, be paired with a proven tom.

When the owner is satisfied that the queen is ready to be mated, she will be placed with the tom. You will need to have proof that your queen is fully covered against the major feline diseases and has tested negative for feline leukemia. In turn, the stud owner will give you similar proof. A repeat mating may be given at no charge should the first one not prove successful. This is not obligatory on the stud owner's behalf so do discuss this at the time of arranging the mating. Commit this to a written contract in order to avoid any misunderstandings later.

The actual mating is a somewhat violent affair, with the male grasping the female by the scruff of the neck and then straddling her. Copulation is very quick in cats, which do not have the lengthy ties seen in dogs. After a short rest the male will mate the female again, and this can be repeated many times over the course of a day.

PREPARING FOR A LITTER

Your Persian can be treated as normal during the early weeks of pregnancy so do not limit her exercise: this is actually very important to her. About three weeks after the mating, her nipples will start to swell and become pink. At this time your vet may be able to confirm pregnancy by palpation of the abdomen. If the litter is small, the queen may show little evidence of pregnancy until it is almost time for the babies to be born. But in most instances there will be a steady swelling of her girth as the embryos develop.

Her appetite will normally start to get bigger due to the nourishment needed by the growing kittens. If she has always been given a well-balanced diet, she will produce strong, healthy kittens and should have no problem producing enough milk for them. You can always sprinkle calcium powder on her food to supply extra amounts of this element, but I would advise this to be done only after consultation with your vet. It may not be necessary. The absorption of calcium is directly related to other elements and vitamins. The concept that more is better just does not hold true.

About three to four weeks before the kittens are due, it would be wise to worm the queen and give her booster vaccinations, so that the kittens start off life with plenty of antibodies in their blood.

It is useful to have a scale for weighing the babies and a supply of old towels and newspapers. A hot water bottle, a pair of scissors, a roll of cotton, and antiseptic lotion should also be kept at hand. As the time approaches for the births, the queen will search for a suitable place. She will be looking for a quiet, dark spot, such as in a linen closet or clothes' drawers and cupboards. She may claw at such places as she tries to prepare a nest.

The best thing is for you to make a kittening box from a sturdy cardboard box. The sides and back should be high enough to provide a sense of security but not so high that she cannot see over them without stretching. The front should be cut down so that she can enter easily, yet be high enough so that the kittens will not be able to clamber out until they are about three weeks old. The bottom can be lined with numerous sheets of paper topped by old towels to make the nest cozy. The box can be placed in one of her favorite spots.

Place the queen in the box in order to try and encourage her to use it in the final days before the birth. If she selects another place

THE BIRTH

In some instances, the first you will know about the birth is when you wake up, or return from work, to find the mother with her babies. However, you will have noted the dates when you would expect the births to take place, based on the date of the mating. The first stage in the birth process is that the queen will go to her box and will probably start to breathe heavily or even pant. A vaginal discharge will then be

A litter of copper-eyed whites. Kittens should never go to their new home before the age of six, preferably eight, weeks.

to have the kittens, then move the box to this site and place the kittens in it. Most mothers will then be satisfied, though they may well move the kittens to other sites over the first few weeks. This is an instinctive behavior pattern of the wild cat, which moves her babies from place to place in order to reduce the chances that a predator might attack the nest.

seen. This period may last for a few hours. The next stage is that the female will start helping the infant into the outside world by bearing down, which means she will voluntarily contract her muscles to help push the baby down the birth canal. This stage can last from a few minutes to an hour or more. However, if it exceeds an hour, it would be wise to phone your vet as there might be a problem.

Assuming this is not the case, the next stage is that you will see the kitten emerging in its membrane. This will be followed by the placenta, which is a mass of jelly-like substance that provided the kitten with nourishment and oxygen as it developed within its mother. Each kitten has its own placenta, other than twins, which may share one. Once the kitten has been expelled, the mother will start to lick it in order to remove the fine membrane in which it is encased. This membrane is filled with a fluid that acted as a sort of cushion to protect the embryo from being jarred or damaged as the mother moved around.

The licking is essential, especially in regard to the membrane over the kitten's mouth, otherwise the kitten would not be able to breathe. The mother will then sever the umbilical cord that connects the kitten to its placenta. She may then start to devour the placenta, or she will leave it while she washes the kitten. The licking process stimulates the infant to cry out as it takes its first breath to fill its lungs with air. It will then find its own way, by crawling, to a nipple.

The time lapse between births can be minutes or hours. In some instances a queen may take a rest of 24 or more hours between births, but as long as she seems content, this is not a problem. Be sure that the placenta is seen after each birth. Should this be retained in the uterus, it could create problems. The mother will usually eat the first placenta or two, which is quite natural. This tissue is full of nutritious food that the mother in the wild would need at this time. However, you can remove any remaining placentas because your Persian is not going to be short of food.

HELPING THE MOTHER

A maiden queen may or may not experience problems when confronted with her first births. Some panic at the sight of their first-born, but thereafter the maternal instinct flows normally with the remainder of the litter. Some may reject most of the first litter, though this would be unusual. If the queen does not know what to do, then you must take an active part in the process. The first thing to do is to carefully pull the membrane away from the mouth of the kitten so it can breathe.

Next, give it a brisk rubbing with a towel while keeping its head in a downward position. This should prompt it to squeal and commence breathing. If not, the next thing is to hold it with its head downward. Now stroke it as though you were milking a cow. This will prompt any fluids in the lungs to be expelled via the mouth, and this should cause the kitten to squeal, thus breathe. Hold the kitten to your ear and listen for any rasping sort of sound, which would suggest that there is still fluid that must be removed. Repeat the process discussed.

The first six weeks or so of a kitten's life are probably the most important in its development.

The toweling will also help to dry the fur so that the kitty does not get chilled. Next you can sever the umbilical cord by using your fingers or scissors. First of all, disinfect a length of cotton and tie it around the cord about one inch from the navel. Now you can cut the cord on the placenta side of the knot. The remaining cord will shrivel up over the next few days. After weighing it, place the kitten with its mother and hopefully her maternal instincts will then take over. She will be very proud of her new baby and any that follow.

CONTACT THE VET

Call your vet at any time during the birth process if the queen is clearly very distressed, is bleeding excessively from the vagina, or has stopped bearing down even though it is clear one or more kittens have yet to be born. If she seems disinterested in the kittens, you should also contact the vet. The queen may not eat for the first day after the births but should regain her appetite later. If not, contact the vet. If any kitten continues to squeal even though it is at a nipple, this again should prompt a talk with the vet. There are, in fact, many things that can go wrong during a birth. It is a case of deciding whether there is an obvious problem with the queen or the infants.

Cream female Persian. Female members of the breed are usually smaller and more restrained than their male counterparts.

REARING THE KITTENS

Once all the babies are born, you can try and tidy up the nest; then leave the mother to fuss over her infants. She will take care of all their needs during the first three weeks. Thereafter you can start to offer them *tiny* pieces of meat, and small amounts of kitten food. Once they are about three to four weeks of age and tottering about, they can be litter trained.

Throughout the early growing weeks, it is wise to weigh the kittens every few days. They should gain weight steadily. Any that do not may have a problem, and the vet should be consulted. Any kittens that are born with deformities may be euthanized by your vet.

Persians are broad and deep through the chest, equally massive across the shoulders and rump, with a well-rounded midsection.

Shaded golden Persian kitten.

EXHIBITING PERSIANS

From the first time cats were seriously exhibited in London in 1871, the cat show has been the very heart of the fancy. It is the place where breeders can have the merits of their stock assessed in a competitive framework, where all cat lovers can meet and discuss ideas, trends and needs, and where new products for cats can be promoted. It is the only event in which you have the opportunity of seeing just about every color and pattern variety that exists in the Persian breed.

Even if you have no plans to become a breeder or exhibitor, you should visit at least one or two cat shows to see what a quality Persian looks like.

The Persian is far and away the most popular exhibition cat and has won more Best in Show awards than any other breed. In Great Britain, about 34 percent of all registered cats are Persians, while in the US the figure is even higher, about 54 percent.

TYPES OF SHOW

Shows range from the small informal affairs that attract a largely local entry to the major all-breed championships and specialty exhibitions that can be spread over two or more days (but only one in Britain). A specialty is a show restricted either by breed or by hair length (short or long). In the US, it is quite common for two or more shows to run concurrently at the same site.

The Persian's large round eyes set wide apart in a large round head contribute to the overall look and expression.

SHOW CLASSES

The number of classes staged at a given show will obviously reflect its size, but the classes fall into various major divisions. These are championships for whole cats, premierships for altered cats, open classes for both of the previous cats, kittens, and household pets. In all but the pet class, there are separate classes for males and females. There are then classes for all of the color and pattern varieties. At a small show, the color/patterns may be grouped into fewer classes than at a major show.

All classes are judged against the standard for the breed, other than pet classes, in which the exhibits are judged on the basis of condition and general appeal, or

Cream Persian kitten.

uniqueness of pattern. An unregistered Persian can be entered into a pet class, and it will be judged on the same basis as would a mixed breed. A kitten in the US is a cat of four months of age but under eight months on the day of a show. In Britain a kitten is a cat of three or more months and under nine months on the show day.

AWARDS AND PRIZES

The major awards in cats are those of Champion and Grand Champion, Premier and Grand Premier. In Britain, a cat must win three challenge certificates under different judges to become a champion, while in the US it must win six winner's ribbons. In both instances, these awards are won via the open class. Once a cat is a champion, it then competes in the champions' class and becomes a grand based on points earned in defeating other champions. The prizes can range from certificates, ribbons and cups to trophies and cash.

Wins in kitten classes do not count toward champion status. Champion status in one association does not carry over to another, in which a cat would have to win its title again based on the rules of that association. The rules of competition are complex, and any would-be exhibitor should obtain a copy of them from their particular registry.

The general format of shows, while differing somewhat from one country to another, are much the same in broad terms. A Persian will enter its color or pattern class. If it wins, it will progress to compete against others in its group (such as self or solid color group, or Himalayan or pointed group). After this, it will meet the other group winners in its breed, and ultimately compete for best of breed and of hair length. If classes have been scheduled for all of the recognized colors and patterns in all of the recognized breeds, then a Best in Show will be the ultimate award.

A show cat comes with a pedigree, which is written documentation of its ancestry tracing back a number of generations. The exact number of generations that are listed on the pedigree varies among cat registries.

JUDGING

As stated earlier, cats are judged against their written standard rather than against each other. A winning cat is one that records the highest total of points, or, put another way, the least number of demerit marks. In the US cats are taken to the judge's table for assessment, but in Britain the judge moves around the pens with a trolley. In the US, judging is done in front of the public, but in the UK judging is normally done before the public is allowed into the hall. The exhibit owners are requested to leave the hall during judging.

CAT PENS

When you arrive at the cat show, a pen will be allocated to your cat. This is an all-wire cage. In Britain, the rules governing what can be placed into the cage are very rigid. This is because there can be no means of identifying the owner of the cat when the judge arrives at that pen. Thus, the blanket, the litter box and the water vessel must all be white. In the US the pens are highly decorated with silks, gorgeous cushions, and so on because the cat is taken to another pen for judging.

THE EXHIBITION PERSIAN

Obviously, a Persian show cat must be a very sound example of

Because show cats are frequently transported over long distances to shows, they are more accustomed to being caged than is the average household pet.

its breed. Its coat must be in truly beautiful condition because the level of competition is extremely high at the major events. At more local affairs, the quality will not be as high, which gives more exhibitors a chance to pick up victories in the absence of the top cats of the country. The male cat must have two descended testicles and have a valid vaccination certificate against feline enteritis that was issued at least seven days before the show. It should have tested negative for feline leukemia (and/or any other diseases as required by your registry).

A show cat must be well-mannered because if it should bite or claw the judge, it is hardly likely to win favor. It could even be disqualified, depending on the regulations of your registry. In any case, such a cat could not be examined properly by the judge, so this alone would preclude it from any hope of winning. It must therefore become accustomed to such treatment by being handled very often as a kitten by friends and relatives.

Black-and-white bi-color Persian. An ideal example of the breed should present an impression of a heavily boned, well-balanced cat with a sweet expression and soft, round lines.

KEEPING YOUR PERSIAN HEALTHY

Like any other animal, your Persian can fall victim to hundreds of diseases and conditions. Most can be prevented by sound husbandry. The majority, should they be recognized in their early stages, can be treated with modern drugs or by surgery. Clearly, preventive techniques are better and less costly than treatments, yet in many instances a cat will become ill because the owner has neglected some basic aspect of general management. In this chapter, we are not so much concerned with cataloging all the diseases your cat could contract, because these are legion, but more concerned with reviewing sound management methods.

HYGIENE

Always apply routine hygiene to all aspects of your pet's management. This alone dramatically reduces the chances of your pet becoming ill because it restricts pathogens (disease-causing organisms) from building up colonies that are able to overcome the natural defense mechanisms of your Persian.

Treats can be provided on an occasional basis to help provide a little variety in the diet. Some treats act as a cleansing agent to help reduce tarter on the cat's teeth. Photo courtesy of Heinz.

1. After your cat has eaten its fill of any moist foods, either discard the food or keep it for later by placing it in your refrigerator. Anything left uneaten at the end of the day can be trashed. Always wash the bowl after each meal. Do not feed your pet from any dishes that are chipped, cracked, or, in the case of plastic, those that are badly scratched.

2. Always store food in a dry, cool cupboard or in the refrigerator in the case of fresh foods.

3. For whatever reason, if you have been handling someone else's cats, always wash your hands before handling your own cats.

4. Be rigorous in cleaning your cat's litter box as soon as you see that it has been fouled.

5. Pay particular attention to the grooming of a Persian cat because so many problems can begin with a seemingly innocuous

event. For example, in itself, a minor cut may not be a major problem as long as it is treated with an antiseptic. But if it is left as an open untreated wound, it is an obvious site for bacterial colonization. The bacteria then gain access to the bloodstream, and a major problem ensues that might not even be associated with the initial wound. The same applies to flea or lice bites. Inspect the skin carefully for signs of flea droppings when you groom a Persian. These appear like minute specks of black dust.

RECOGNIZING AN ILL CAT

You must be able to recognize when your cat is ill in order to seek a solution to the problem. You must learn to distinguish between a purely temporary condition and one that will need some form of veterinary advice and/or treatment. For example, a cat can sprain a muscle by jumping and landing awkwardly. This would normally correct itself over a 36-48 hour period. Your pet may contract a slight chill, or its feces might become loose. Both conditions will normally correct themselves over a day or so. On the other hand, if a condition persists for more than two days, it would be advisable to telephone your vet for advice.

In general, any appearance or behavior that is not normal for your cat would suggest something is responsible for the abnormality. This is your first indication that something may be amiss. The following are a number of signs that indicate a problem:

1. Diarrhea, especially if it is very liquid, foul-smelling or blood-streaked. If blood is seen in the urine, this is also an indication of a problem, as is excessive straining or cries of pain when the cat tries to relieve itself.

2. Discharge from the nose or eyes. Many Persians may discharge a liquid from the eyes due to blocked tear ducts. This is associated with the foreshortening of the muzzle. However, an excessive discharge needs veterinary attention.

3. Repeated vomiting. All cats are sick occasionally with indigestion. They will also vomit after eating grass, but repeated vomiting is not normal.

4. Wheezing sounds when breathing, or any other suggestion of breathing difficulties.

5. Excessive scratching. All cats will have a good scratch on a quite regular basis, but excessive scratching indicates a skin problem, especially if it has created sores or lesions.

6. Constant rubbing of the rear end along the ground.

7. Bald patches, lesions, cuts, and swellings on the body, legs, tail, or face.

8. The coat seems to lack bounce or life, and is dull.

9. The cat is listless and lethargic, showing little interest in what is going on around it.

10. The eyes have a glazed look to them, or the haw (nictitating membrane, or third eyelid) is clearly visible.

11. The cat is displaying an unusual lack of interest in its favorite food items.

this group, two of them are especially dangerous. They are feline viral rhinotracheitis (FVR) and feline calicivirus (FCV). The vaccination for the prevention of these diseases is combined and given when the kitten is six or more weeks of age; a booster follows three to four weeks later.

Feline leukemia virus complex (FeLV): This disease was first recognized in 1964, and a vaccine became available in the US in about 1985. Like "cat flu," the name is misleading, because it is far more complex than a blood cancer, which is what its name implies. Essentially, it destroys the cat's immune system, so the cat may contract any of the major diseases.

Good husbandry will go a long way in helping to keep your Persian in good health.

The disease is easily spread via the saliva of a cat as it licks other cats. It is also spread prenatally from an infected queen to her offspring via the blood, or when washing her kittens. This is why it is important to test all breeding cats for FeLV. Vaccination is worthwhile only on a kitten or cat that has tested negative. If a cat tests positive for the disease, it has a 70 percent chance of survival, though it will be a carrier in many instances.

Feline infectious peritonitis (FIP): This disease has various effects on the body's metabolism. There are no satisfactory tests for it, but intranasal liquid vaccinations via a dropper greatly reduce the potential for it to develop in the tissues of the nose.

PARASITES

Parasites are organisms that live on or in a host. They feed from it without providing any benefit in return. External parasites include fleas, lice, ticks, flies, and any other creature that bites the skin of the cat. Internal parasites include all pathogens, but the term is more commonly applied to worms in their various forms.

External parasites and their eggs can be seen with the naked eye. All can be eradicated with treatment from your vet. However, initial treatment will need to be followed by further treatments because most compounds are ineffective on the eggs. The repeat treatments kill the larvae as they hatch. It is also important that all bedding be treated or destroyed because this is often where parasites prefer to live when not on the host.

All cats are host to a range of worm species. If worms multiply in the cat, they adversely affect its health. They will cause loss of appetite, wasting, and a steady deterioration in health. At a high level of infestation, they may be seen in the fecal matter, but normally it will require fecal microscopy by your vet. This will establish the species and the relative density of the eggs, thus the level of infestation.

Treatment is normally via tablets, but liquids are also available. Because worms are so common, the best husbandry technique is to routinely treat breeding cats for worms prior to their being bred, then for the queen and her kittens to be treated periodically.

The Persian's thick, long coat can be a perfect hiding place for fleas and other parasites. Check your pet regularly for any signs of infestation.

Discuss a testing and treatment program with your vet.

NEUTERING AND SPAYING

Desexing your cat is normally done when a female is about four months of age and somewhat later with a male. The operation is quite simple with a male but more complicated with a female. It is still a routine procedure. It is possible to delay estrus in a breeding queen, but the risk of negative side effects makes this a dubious course to take. Discuss it with your vet. A cat of any age can be neutered (male) or spayed (female); but if they are adults, they take some months (especially males) before they lose their old habits.

FIRST AID

Although you might think that such inquisitive creatures as cats would be prone to many physical injuries, this is not actually the case. They usually extricate themselves from dangerous situations because of their very fast reflexes. However, injuries do happen, and the most common is caused by the cat darting across a road and being hit by a vehicle. About 40 percent of cats die annually due to traffic accidents. The next level of injury will be caused by cats getting bitten or scratched when fighting among themselves, or being bitten by an insect, or by a sharp object getting lodged in their fur or feet.

Words with **or, ore**

Look at each picture. Read the words.

or
ore

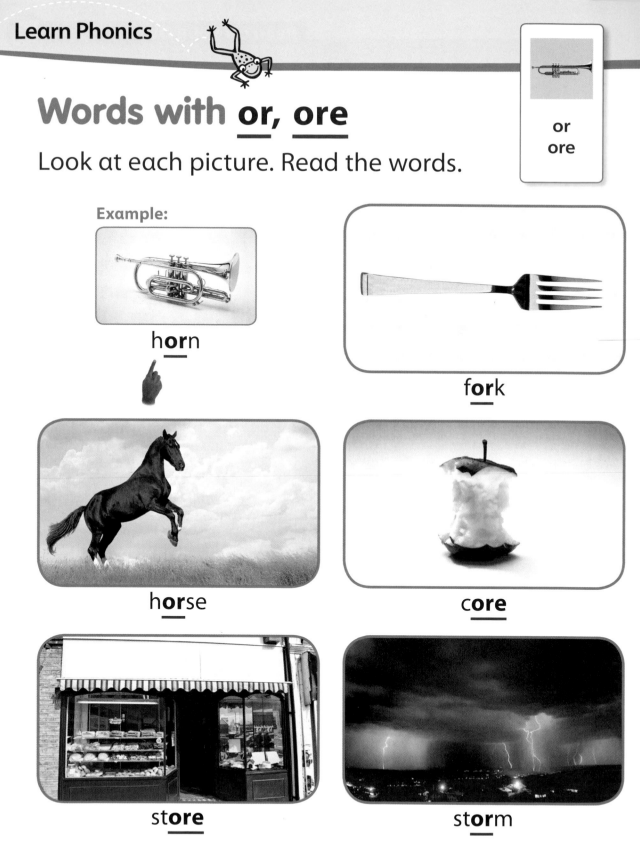

Example:

h**or**n

f**or**k

h**or**se

c**ore**

st**ore**

st**or**m

High Frequency Words
after
better
buy
idea
pull
until

Key Words

Look at the pictures.
Read the sentences.

Horses or Cars?

1. **Until** people started to **buy** cars, many people used horses.

2. Horses could **pull** carts.

3. People drove to more places **after** they had cars.

4. They thought driving was a **better idea**.

Do you think cars are better than horses? Why?

Phonics Games
NGReach.com

3

Before and After the Car

by Lorna Shore

Before people had cars, they walked.

They used horses, boats, bikes, or trains.

People used horses to pull carts, too.

After people had cars, they drove.

Henry Ford

In 1900, cars cost a lot, so not many people owned cars. Henry Ford was one of many people who made cars at the start of the 1900s. Ford wanted more people to buy his cars.

Model T

Ford had an idea. He would make a car for a low price. Then more people could buy it. In 1908, Ford made the Model T. People paid $850 for this car.

Model T

People drove other sorts of cars, too, but more and more drove Model T cars. They liked its price. By 1927, Ford had sold more than 15,000,000 Model T cars.

Until there were cars, people didn't pave many roads. But if a road wasn't paved, it turned to mud in rainstorms. This was bad for cars.

paved road

Cars needed better roads. So, people started paving more roads. Paved roads did not turn into mud in storms.

city

The car changed where people could live. Before cars, people who worked in a city had to live in that city. Now they could drive to work. Groups of homes sprang up around a city.

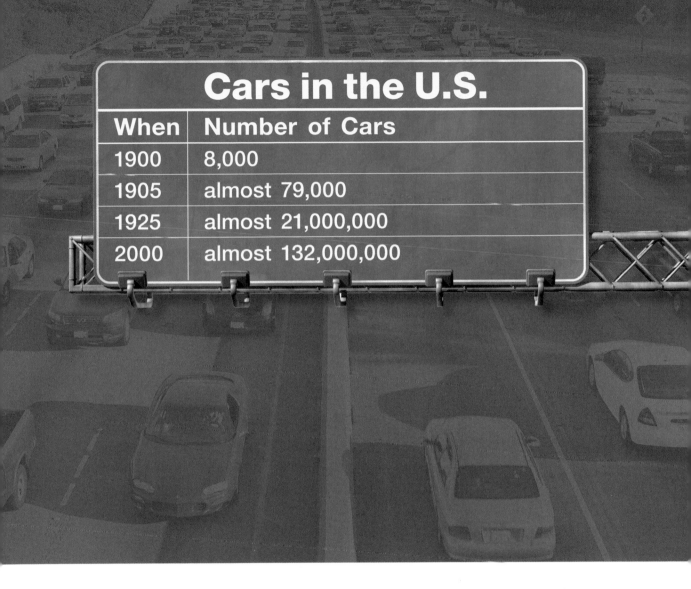

Cars in the U.S.	
When	**Number of Cars**
1900	8,000
1905	almost 79,000
1925	almost 21,000,000
2000	almost 132,000,000

As time passed, more people drove cars. The chart shows how the number of cars in the U.S. has changed from 1900 to 2000.

Today people drive on roads from their homes to stores. They drive to the shore. Many cars fill the roads. ❖

Words with or, ore

Read these words.

for	horse	sort	storm	fort
drove	road	car	store	shore

Find the words with **or** and **ore**.
Use letters to build them.

f o r

Talk Together

Where is the _horse_ ?

Choose words from the box above to talk about the pictures.

The _horse_ is by the _shore_.

Syllables

Look at each picture. Read the words.

Example:

insect

banjo

muffin

ostrich

window

pillow

bedspread

bedroom

High Frequency Words

after
better
buy
idea
pull
until

Key Words

Look at the picture. Read the ad.

We Buy Ideas!

1. The ad said: We will **buy** your **idea**!
2. Can you think of a **better** way to **pull** things?
3. Test your idea **after** you think of it.
4. Don't send us your idea **until** it works.

> What things do you pull?

Phonics Games

NGReach.com

15

A Contest for Carmen

by Tory Wren • illustrated by Amanda Haley

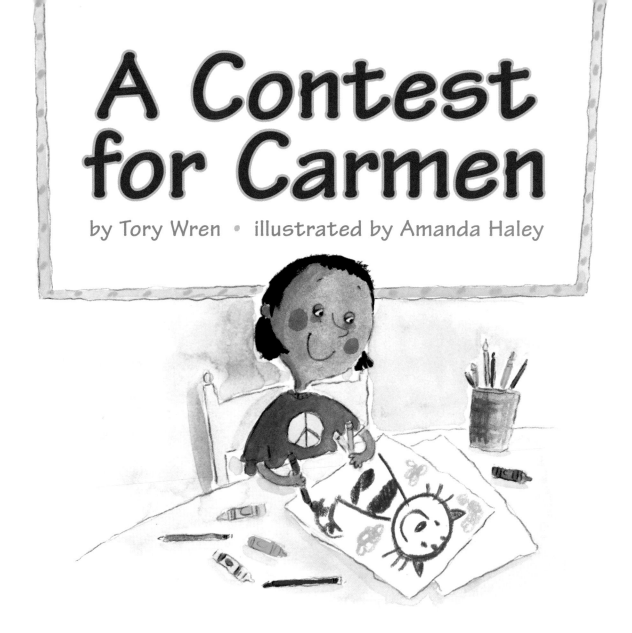

Carmen liked to invent things.

She wanted to make life better for people.

Carmen liked to make people happy, too.

So she liked to draw funny cartoons.

One day after lunch, Carmen was
reading in her bedroom. She saw an ad
for a contest.

This is what the ad said:

CONTEST!

Make the World a **Better Place**

How would you make the world a better place? What would you invent? Send us your idea by March 25.

"I have five days to think of a winning idea," said Carmen. Then she started to draw. Carmen had many ideas. She drew cartoons until it was bedtime.

Carmen drew a cartoon of plastic
mittens with wool lining. They kept hands
warm. And they didn't get wet in the rain
or snow.

She drew a picnic basket. It fit into a pocket. People could carry it with them in case they got hungry.

One day Carmen got this e-mail.

FROM: Make the World a Better Place
SUBJECT: Contest
DATE: June 2
TO: Carmen Mendez

You did not win the contest, but your cartoons made us happy. May we buy them from you?

Syllables

Read these words.

picnic	drew	bedroom	dentist	duckling
bunny	invent	muffin	sandwich	hoped

Find the words with more than one syllable. Use letters to build them.

p i c n i c

Choose words from the box above to tell your partner about the cartoon.

I see a _bunny_ at the picnic.

25

Go to the Shore!

Help the car drive to the shore fast. Trace the path with your finger. The following steps give you an idea of the route to take.

1. Go past the muffin store to the traffic light.
2. Go up.

3. Pass the horse trying to pull a truck.
4. Go down after the horse.
5. Pass the sandwich shop. Do not stop to buy a sandwich!
6. Follow the road until you reach the shore.

Acknowledgments
Grateful acknowledgment is given to the authors, artists, photographers, museums, publishers, and agents for permission to reprint copyrighted material. Every effort has been made to secure the appropriate permission. If any omissions have been made or if corrections are required, please contact the Publisher.

Photographic Credits
CVR (Cover) Jaren Wicklund/iStockphoto. **2** (bl) PhotoDisc/Getty Images. (br) Creatas/Jupiterimages. (cl) pirita/Shutterstock. (cr) MetaTools. (tl) PhotoDisc/Getty Images. (tr) Artville. **3** (b) Liz Garza Williams/Hampton-Brown/National Geographic School Publishing. (tl) Jupiterimages/Getty Images. (tr) DigitalStock/Corbis. **4** (b) Stefan Klein/iStockphoto. (inset) Bettmann/Corbis. (t) Ayaaz Rattansi/iStockphoto. **5** Bettmann/Corbis. **6** Bettmann/Corbis. **7** Bettmann/Corbis. **8** Minnesota Historical Society/Corbis. **9** Stefan Klein/iStockphoto. (inset) H. Armstrong Roberts/ClassicStock/Corbis. **10** (bg) Margaret Bourke-White/Getty Images. (inset) Hulton-Deutsch Collection/Corbis. **11** (bg) Digital Vision/PunchStock. (fg) Geoffrey Holman/iStockphoto. **12** wendy connett/Alamy Images. **13** (b) Liz Garza Williams/Hampton-Brown/National Geographic School Publishing. (cl) Eline Spek/Shutterstock. (cr) Panoramic Images/Getty Images. (t) Liz Garza Williams/Hampton-Brown/National Geographic School Publishing. **14** (b) Stephanie Swartz/iStockphoto. (cl) Artville. (cr) Digital Vision/Getty Images. (tl) MetaTools. (tr) Artville. **15** (b) Liz Garza Williams/Hampton-Brown/National Geographic School Publishing. (t) Somos/Veer/Getty Images. **18** PhotoDisc/Getty Images. **25** (t) Liz Garza Williams/Hampton-Brown/National Geographic School Publishing.

Illustrator Credits
16-24 Amanda Haley. **25-27** Jackie Stafford

The National Geographic Society
John M. Fahey, Jr., President & Chief Executive Officer
Gilbert M. Grosvenor, Chairman of the Board

National Geographic School Publishing
Hampton-Brown
www.NGSP.com

Printed in the USA.
RR Donnelley, Jefferson City, MO

ISBN: 978-0-7362-8047-1

12 13 14 15 16 17 18 19
10 9 8 7 6 5 4

after
better
buy
idea
pull
until

Target Sound/Spellings

r-Controlled Vowels <u>or</u>, <u>ore</u>	Syllables
Selection: **Before and After the Car** before for Ford horse(s) more or rainstorms shore sorts stores storms	**Selection:** **A Contest for Carmen** basket bedroom bedtime bunny Carmen carry cartoon(s) contest funny happy hopping hungry invent mittens picnic plastic subject winning